CW00376372

And empower you to have the life you always wanted

This Book WILL Change Your Life

'And empower you to have the life you always wanted'

And empower you to have the life you always wanted

This Book WILL Change Your Life

'And empower you to have the life you always wanted'

Published by Steve Wharton

Wolviston, TS22 5LP, England

ISBN 9798838120045

Copyright © stevewharton2022

A CIP record is available for this book from the British Library

The moral right of the author has been asserted

Printed in Great Britain by Steve Wharton

—

6

And empower you to have the life you always wanted

CONTENTS

And empower you to have the life you always wanted

Introduction

'You must be the change you wish to see in the world'
-Mahatma Ghandi

It's actually very easy to change your life.

All you have to do is understand in a simple way what is going on inside of you and then have an easy to implement practice to follow, that will change what is going on inside of you.

This is because the life you are immersed in and experiencing is a direct reflection of what is inside of you, so to change the outside you need to change the inside. I know to some this may sound a little far fetched but if you do some research you will soon find many revered teachings confirming this line of thought, even Buddha said this over 2500 years ago:

'Since everything is a reflection of our minds, everything can be changed by our minds'.
-Buddha

So let's get started, coming back to the present times all across the world right now all we seem to hear about is 'mental health' it has become one of the hottest topics of this era.

—

And it appears just about everyone is suffering from it in one way or another with new problems being identified and labelled virtually by the day. It is fast becoming a global health crisis which appears to be out of control and the world it appears is struggling to cope.

I am not disagreeing with this assessment however I believe in general the answer is not so complicated and this 'mental health crisis' that affects all of us can be turned around if we understand and approach it in the right way and when we do that our lives will change dramatically for the better.

So the more people that gain a simple understanding of why this is happening and how it can be corrected the better because this is the core controlling factor that determines every aspect of your life. And of course some mental health problems may be due to conditions not covered by this approach but in general I believe the solution given in this mini-book will help in the majority of cases.

So before I explain what this 'mental health crisis' really is and then look at how changing what's going on inside of you is the solution, I want to alter your perspective slightly and give you an alternative way to view it all.

Chapter 1

'If you want to find the secrets of the Universe, think in terms of energy, frequency and vibration'.
-Dr Nicola Tesla

So what is really going on?

The first thing I would like you to understand is that you live in a world that is in fact made of energy. Yes that's right everything you see around you including your physical body is actually made from energy, which in its basic form is atoms, microscopic atoms that are pulsing and vibrating.

The house you live in, the car you drive, trees, furniture, food, animals etc are all made up from these tiny atoms, any scientist or physicist will confirm this. So if you are made from energy (atoms) and all energy vibrates then at some level you must be vibrating? This is correct; you are constantly vibrating even though you can't directly sense this happening, although you can indirectly sense it through the fluctuation of your moods as you go through your day. One minute you may be happy and feeling joyful the next you may get some bad news and suddenly feel down and depressed.

—

This happens all the time as you encounter the ups and down's of everyday life. This is you sensing your energy vibration, through the way that you feel. When you feel good you are vibrating fast and when you feel bad your energy vibration is slowing down.

That makes sense because fast vibrating feelings are joy, excitement, happiness, peacefulness and love etc and slow vibrating feelings are anger, fear, anxiety, depression, jealousy, greed etc. So the spectrum range of feelings goes from fast vibrating 'love' down to slow vibrating 'fear' with all the variations in between.

So you can see how it works and why everyday of your life you experience many different positive and negative feelings as you ride up and down on the vibrational roller coaster ride we call life. It's a muti-vibrational energy experience in every sense of the word and the reason I want you to understand that is because this makes it easier to accept the next chapter which is all about your emotions and how they play a massive role in determining the life you have.

'Everything is energy and that's all there is to it. Match the frequency of the reality you want and you cannot help but get that reality. It can be no other way'.
-Albert Einstein

—

Chapter 2

'90% of all the pain we experience is due to emotional baggage, trapped emotions and those energies stay with us and cause much of our diseases and self-sabotage'.
-Dr Bradley Nelson
(The Emotion Code)

Trapped emotions

Next I want you to understand how you get compromised and in effect programmed by your immediate environment through the different emotional energies that you encounter.

Generally this involuntary programming happens more in the first seven years of your life when you are very receptive to what's going on around you and acting like a sponge in terms of readily soaking up the energies that you are subjected to.

So when you are in the vicinity of other people who have powerful emotional moments like heated arguments filled with anger and frustration some of the energy generated unfortunately becomes absorbed by you. And this can leave you with some of that emotional energy trapped inside of you, which builds up and adds to the residue that you have already accumulated.

—

Eventually these 'stuck emotions' will begin manifesting through you, causing you to develop instinctive reactions when similar circumstances pop up again.

In other words you automatically start behaving in a similar way solidifying the trapped emotions even further in the process.

This is how your personality begins to form and this is all part of you being molded by your life experiences into the person you will be.

When the bulk of the energy you are experiencing is predominantly negative, which is usually the case as currently it is estimated that the average person's thoughts are 80% negative in nature, it can become the dominant energy form displayed by you, manifesting in a number of different ways.

Such as making you prone to angry outbursts, mood swings, violent behaviour, sulks, addictive tendencies, severe bouts of anxiety, depression, argumentative, self-pitying, antagonistic, bullying, self-harming, arrogant, vindictive, predatory etc.

Plus many more negative behaviour patterns and traits that humans can display.

13

When this is the case essentially this means you have become stuck in the lower vibrations and this energy spectrum is generally where you will spend the majority of your life because it will be constantly manifesting from inside of you as it gets triggered day after day.

The negativity you carry within determines where (vibrationally) you will spend most of your time and ultimately your life.

This is the major factor that defines you and determines how difficult your life path will be and a lower vibrational type of upbringing would certainly be very influential in making you a more negatively minded person and potentially lead to a more unhappy life filled with problems.

The accumulated trapped emotions would effectively be holding you at a slower more negative vibration. And you would then experience the corresponding life.

On the other hand if you grow up in a loving, joyful, happy home with lots of positive energies around such as joy, fun, thoughtfulness, caring, love etc then you will generally download and become used to these types of energies and this will be the energy spectrum that you from then on usually display and spend the majority of your time in.

—

14

From this you can see how important your parents are and how fortunate you are if you have high vibrational parents with little inner negativity to pass on down to you.

This ensures that you will tend to be in general more positive in nature and your life will have much more chance of being happy and content.

Its no coincidence that many people that have a loving positive upbringing go on to have successful and happy lives, they have less getting in the way.

They are fortunate enough to be carrying a smaller less influential and damaging ball of inner negativity, so in effect they have ended up with fewer inner demons to contend with.

Like energy attracts like energy so dependant on the amount of inner negativity you have accumulated determines what you will naturally draw into your life, the type of partner, job, friends, wealth, health etc.

So in general what is inside of you is what you gravitate to on the outside. The more trapped emotions you are carrying the more you will attract people and circumstances with a similar amount.

And although you pick up many of your trapped emotions during the hyper sensitive early years you also pick them up as you go through your life, especially when you have highly charged intense emotional experiences such as going through a divorce, job loss, breakups, serious accidents, serious illness, bereavement etc, so as you can see it's an ongoing process.

And when you have one of these highly charged intense emotional experiences it can be so distressing that you may suffer what is referred to as PTSD (Post traumatic stress disorder), which basically means you have experienced a severe drop in vibration due to the severity of what you have been through.

Or put another way you have suddenly taken on board an unprecedented and large amount of slow vibrating negative energy and this has plunged or dragged you down the vibrations, leaving you stuck even further down than usual in an extreme negative state.

This is when you may see a person really struggle to maintain their lives, which could lead to homelessness, alcoholism, drug addiction, a fall into crime; relationship breakdowns, serious ill health etc, and in a worst case scenario even suicidal tendencies.

—

The exceptional drop in vibration is just too much to cope with and they desperately need to find relief from the overwhelming and foreboding feelings that are now engulfing them.

If you find yourself trapped in the lower vibrations you will experience the energies that exist there and the further down you are the worse it is and this will spill out infecting every area of your life.

You are a totally different person depending on where your vibration has settled and this is why we see many people who are trapped down here behaving in ways that may seem massively out of character.

They cannot help how they act because they are now essentially a totally different person and the majority of us would be influenced to behave in exactly the same way if we were in their shoes.

So please don't be too quick to judge others because you don't really know where they are vibrationally and they may well be trapped in a very difficult state of mind through no fault of their own and need all the help, love and understanding they can get to overcome this.

They need help to get them back up the vibrations and this is easier said than done.

—

Chapter 3

'Let's raise children who won't have to recover from their childhoods'
-Pam Leo
An independent scholar in human development, a parent educator, a certified childbirth educator, a doula, a parent, and a grandparent

Mental health

Now let's look at how this affects your mental health.

Accumulating a residue of negative energy is just part of life and something that you have to contend with. Everyone has it; some only have a small amount and others a large overpowering amount.

Essentially this is the after effects of all the traumas small or large that you have faced and gone through, from the extreme example of a loveless abusive childhood to something that may be perceived as less damaging such as someone calling you names, or maybe just been involved in a severe heated argument, losing a loved one, having a serious accident, suffering neglect, rejection, ill health etc. I could go on and on there are endless examples.

—

And empower you to have the life you always wanted

These traumas and mini-traumas can take many forms and we have all experienced them many times over and this is what has left us with trapped negative emotions.

And this is what I believe causes the majority of mental health problems.

Remove your inner negativity or inner demons and you would remove the majority of mental health issues that human beings suffer from.

In fact existing in this state of being where you are heavily influenced by your inner negativity has become so 'normal', so accepted that most of the time you don't even realise its happening.

You only think that the people who are seriously malfunctioning are the ones with problems but that is not the case we are all affected all of the time to some degree. And in general we manage to stumble through our lives carrying this burden without giving too much attention to it.

However we could all have a much better life if we sorted this problem out and were able to release some of this negativity. This would allow us to rise in vibration and live our lives in a higher vibrational state where negative energy would not be able to play havoc with and hurt us so much.

—

And empower you to have the life you always wanted

Unfortunately for some who are carrying a lot of negativity it can become unbearable and it does so much damage they have a miserable life full of problems and dramas, I am sure we all know many people like that.

When you are carrying a lot of negativity it flares up constantly, powerfully infecting your life and the lives of others around you.

The symptoms of carrying a strong powerful dose of negative energy varies from person to person. It may make one person act as a bully, another could suffer from depression and another may end up hooked on drugs or alcohol or even experience lots of ill health. It all depends on your personality traits, your genes and the behaviour patterns you have been exposed to.

And you could even grow up with a brother or sister and they seem unphased by that same upbringing whereas you are devastated by it. Everybody is different and we all react differently to our experiences it's not an exact science but generally this is how it works.

The bottom line is the ball of trapped negative energy that we all have stuck within us is what is causing the majority of our problems. And it constantly replenishes itself topping up its battery when it surges through us.

This is how it stays charged up and strong by every now and again flaring up. And when this happens you become that energy, like when you feel a surge of anger and become angry or when you feel yourself sinking down into misery and become depressed. It is controlling you and you think it's you but it's not you, it is the trapped emotions you have stuck inside of you living through you.

Another way to understand this trapped energy is to picture it as a little gremlin inside of you; you can even give it a name and as I said previously the bigger and more powerful it is the more havoc it will be creating in your life. The prisons and mental institutions are full of people with powerful inner gremlins.

The gremlin is why a person who bullies people is never satisfied they always need to move on to the next person to bully because their gremlin needs more negative emotional energy, it wants its food and if it doesn't keep getting replenished it will fizzle away so its always seeking the next opportunity.

In truth it's the gremlin that's bullying people not so much the bully, the gremlin is the driving force behind the bully's cruel actions. Take the gremlin away and the bully would stop bullying people.

—

21

The same applies to the depressed person, the drug addict, the alcoholic, the person who self-harms or has anxiety issues etc.

It's the repetitive and never ending routine of satisfying the gremlin within that always needs its next fix, which it gets through your negative emotions.

When you feel guilty, angry, sad, worthless, jealous, depressed, unloved, self-pitying etc you are feeding your inner gremlin and it gets you to feel like this by encouraging you to drink, take drugs, bully someone, feel jealous, hate yourself, hate others etc.

Whatever way it has found works best to get you in a negative emotional state it will constantly use to feed on the emotions this generates within you. It negatively taints your thinking because it is there; if it is part of you, it will infect you. And it will learn how to push the exact buttons it knows will do the job and you will then automatically react giving it what it wants every time.

Yes it is even said it carries a primitive form of intelligence and knows how to intentionally manipulate you and encourage you into negative mindsets; as I pointed out previously many ancient teachings refer to this inner energy source as your inner demons and there are many stories of people being driven to despair by them.

—

And their greatest strength is you not knowing they are there but not anymore because now you know.

Now you are empowered with the knowledge of how it works and this is the first important step in you gaining control.

The fact that you now understand how it works and can acknowledge the presence of your inner demons puts you back in the driving seat.

Awareness of their presence is the key because this is what shifts your mind to a much more empowering perspective.

This enables you to recognise their promptings when they occur and this is a vital step on the road to you finally releasing them for good.

There is no going back now that you are equipped with this knowledge and its time to give notice to the parasites that have covertly been sabotaging your life.

Chapter 4

'I am absolutely convinced it is our trapped emotions and traumas and anxieties and unprocessed life experiences that we hold in our nervous system that is the source of everything that ails us'.
-Sonia Choquette
(Founder of 6th Sensory Living and Author)

Summary

So let's presume you are born basically pure and negative energy free (although it is thought you may also carry some negativity from your experiences within the womb or even passed on down through your genes) then it all begins as you enter your family environment and experience negative emotional flare ups from your parents and siblings. This subjects you to those energies and as you process them some of the residue becomes trapped within you and you are then on the way to forming your own ball of inner negativity or your own inner gremlin.

Then when you have enough of this energy stuck inside of you its influence causes you to start having negative emotional flare ups and you are then adding to the mix of energies in your immediate environment.

This means you have become part of the cycle damaging yourself and others in your close vicinity.

This is why it is so important to bring children up in the best possible energy spectrum as the pathways they will take in their lives literally is in general determined by the early years energy that they spend their time in.

And because of this phenomenon everybody is essentially suffering from 'mental illness' to some degree and for some it's not too bad even acceptable but for others it's intolerable.

This without doubt is the most powerful overriding factor that we have to contend with in our lives, it affects literally everything and I mean everything, our relationships, work life, the amount of success we can achieve, our health etc, nothing is untouched by this.

So the cure is obvious 'get rid of what is causing the problem' and that is the negative energy each of us is carrying within, the alien that has took up residence.

Then you would rise in vibration and your life would be changed instantly and massively for the better in every conceivable way.

You see the higher the vibration that you can attain the more happiness, joy, fun, good fortune and love etc you will experience in your life. You are a different and much more positively orientated person when you exist at a higher vibration.

Everything seems to work out for the better and things just go your way and you are less bothered by the problems of life because you have less negativity inside of you blowing it all out of proportion.

It's as if you can simply let the relentless daily niggles go without buying into them and when you are in a higher vibrational state this all comes quite naturally to you.

You will of course still have your ups and downs but much less severe in terms of the damage you suffer than if you were continuously dragged down by the burden of a heavier slow vibrating powerful ball of inner negativity.

I also feel that you need to be careful of extensive therapy digging into the past to find out why someone has 'mental health' issues as a method of releasing them, because this can sometimes simply regurgitate the pain and suffering, which could potentially leave you with even more powerful inner demons than before.

It makes more sense to me to accept the fact that we have damage (everybody does) and simply focus on releasing that pain (negative energy) using techniques that are designed to do that.

Everyone goes through stuff which in general is unknowingly inflicted upon them by people who are behaving that way because they are damaged themselves, so why not just focus on getting rid of that stuck energy and concentrate on healing.

I feel its not about 'who done what to me' because we all got damaged, its more productive to accept that unfortunately it has happened and concentrate on getting rid of it (the stuck energy), it's just part of the experience that we call life.

Nobody would knowingly hurt you if they carried no inner pain themselves, they are also suffering and it's their inner pain that causes them to lash out and behave in ways that may hurt others.

Realising this and detaching from the negativity involved is the answer, so take your thoughts away from anyone that may have hurt you and let them get on with it, they have their own path to tread and lessons to learn. Dwelling on it keeps you stuck in the pain so it's best for you to let it go and move on.

If you get caught up in negative thoughts and feelings such as seeking revenge or falling into the habit of churning over what they did to you, you are fuelling your inner negativity, you are feeding it.

This kind of mindset is only hurting you more and if you persist in this line of thought it could grow even stronger giving it more influence over you.

Then it will most certainly cause more chaos and damage in your life.

The key is learning how to let go, and this is of course very difficult to master but with a sound practice to follow and discipline you can defeat the monster within and claim back control of your life.

This is the battle between the dark and the light and coming to the realisation that this all takes place within you is truly a momentous step in your spiritual journey.

Chapter 5

'Many of the things that are pushed upon the masses creates negative emotional molecules, once they are formed they are real and you can't get them out of your body unless you know how'.
-Don Tolman
Whole Foods Nutritionist and Author

Removing trapped emotions

I am going to give you one excellent practice to follow that will help you release your inner negativity and at the end of the book you will find references to other techniques and books which you can research yourself, in fact just Google 'removing trapped emotions' and plenty of good information will come up.

It's well worth trying different methods to find what suits you best.

The method I recommend is called 'visualising your inner lake' and the purpose of this technique is to train yourself to focus on something positive and serene at all times but especially when your ball of inner negativity sparks into life.

You must learn to become the master of your emotions instead of them mastering you. And the skill you must cultivate to do this is falling into a state of surrender and that means completely accepting whatever is happening without buying into any emotional surges that may be tugging at you, no anger, frustration, annoyance, exasperation etc, you must train yourself to hold your inner peace at all times.

You must unlearn what you have thus far been trained to automatically do; you must control your inbuilt instinctive emotional reactions to events when they unfold. So you settle into your serenity by following the visualisation and hold it even when you are buffeted by negative energies vying for your attention.

This is the key to mastering control and when you do this successfully you will be whittling away at your inner negativity because every time you manage to remain detached from it when it is clawing at you, you release some of it, so it is effectively shrinking.

"Your task is not to seek for love, but merely to seek and find all the barriers within yourself that you have built against it."
-Rumi
13th century Persian poet

—

Here is a simple visualisation to help you achieve this.

Picture a beautiful turquoise blue lake inside your chest; imagine for the moment the surface of the water is slightly disturbed; this is caused by waves of negative energy pulsing outwards from your ever active inner ball of negativity.

This creates a rippling across the surface which intensifies when something stressful occurs or when your thoughts drift towards the negative, or even when somebody brings negative energy into your immediate surroundings through their mood and presence.

Now I want you to take a few slow deep breaths and see the water becoming perfectly still not a ripple upon the surface just a flicker of glistening sunlight bouncing off the now calm and perfectly still lake.

Hold that beautiful image and continue taking slow deep breaths.

As you gently focus on your breathing I want you to feel the stillness this beautiful image evokes within you, sense the tranquility and let it wash over you. This is your inner peace and serenity that you are now picturing and feeling; bask in this moment for twenty to thirty seconds as you focus on your breathing.

During your day remember to occasionally take a deep breath especially if you sense inner turmoil stirring to bring you instantly back to the calm still lake. This will hone your skill at detaching from any negativity when it arises.

keep practicing going back to the stillness and you will soon master this little exercise.

This is what you must learn, initially calming the waters and then holding the picture of the calm still lake within and the feeling of serenity it generates, no matter what is happening on the outside. I often relax close my eyes and imagine I am visiting my lake, I might see myself sitting on a deck chair at the waters edge for a while watching the ebb and flow of the water or maybe drifting in a rowing boat enjoying the peace and tranquility.

The more you practice this type of visualisation the better you will get at doing it and before long you will be able to walk through your day undisturbed by all the never ending mayhem that takes place around you because you will be able to bask in the peace and serenity generated by the image of your inner lake. You will have trained yourself to settle into the eye of the storm and the sense of inner peace this generates will be gently bubbling up from inside of you.

Mastering the mindset of serenity whilst walking in the never ending chaos will help you to release your inner ball of negativity because each time you manage to hold your inner peace and not become angry, irritated, stressed, worried, frustrated, anxious etc you will be breaking it down and letting some of it go.

This is a spiritual practice and something that you should always be trying to incorporate into your thought process because when you focus on this image and the associated feelings your vibration will rise and that means whatever you are doing in your regular everyday life will improve. This is because you have lifted up your vibration and are holding it there while you go about your everyday tasks and this will ensure better results for you.

This is what is often referred to as 'getting into the zone' and many sports professionals follow practices like this to hold their vibration up because it allows them to achieve peak performance. It does not stop you going about your daily business and doing what you have to do but it does quieten your normally ever chattering conscious mind and lift your vibration and this is a much better mindset to be in than a head swirling with negative thoughts and feelings, which is what most people are habitually experiencing.

———

Just look around at peoples faces and more often than not they look distracted and unhappy and this has become 'the norm'.

What you can see is an active ball of inner negativity on auto pilot gnawing away at them through their thoughts and feelings. As you progress with this practice you will notice you become less and less involved in arguments and disagreements. It's as if you no longer feel the need to be right or to win because you are more focused on holding the feeling of detachment from potential negative feelings rather than proving someone else wrong, regardless of whether they are or not.

It doesn't matter any more and you embody this state of mind, the peaceful serenity that this evokes overrides whatever happens in the emotional tussles taking place. You can still have robust discussions but they are now devoid of the negative emotional charge that previously overshadowed proceedings.

And after a while you will see these episodes become less and less in your life and this is when you will ponder the utter futility of getting into an emotionally charged disagreement with somebody as you naturally take on an altogether higher perspective. A view point from above the ego level so to speak.

And this is when you will also realise its not really about forgiving somebody who you feel may have wronged you but more an absolute letting go of the energy charge surrounding the whole situation.

Stepping aside from the emotionally charged energy is the key and pivotal in achieving this is not allowing yourself to be drawn into any kind of judgment or need to be right.

'It doesn't matter' is the mantra and this detached approach is the secret mind hack to releasing the remaining residue of trapped emotions that you still carry.

Forgiving somebody generally means you are still holding onto the belief that they have done something wrong to you, this is you still buying into the energy charge at some level, when completely letting go of that energy charge is what's needed.

So it's not so much forgiveness it's more letting go that allows you to release the trapped emotions. 'Let them keep their pain' is the way forward and this approach allows you to break free.

This is the key to you taking back control from your inner negativity that has up until this point had a free reign in respect of the powerful influence it has exerted over you.

And this will allow you to move up in vibration, which is the secret to really changing your life.

As Lao Tzu so eloquently puts it releasing your trapped negative emotions is the greatest gift you can give to the world because this changes you into a higher vibrational person and then you automatically help others by the example you have become.

Or to put it another way you help others by the energy vibration that you now exist at because just being in your company will give them an energy boost. A quick buzz as they hitch a lift up in vibration by simply being in your presence. This will of course wear off for them as their inner negativity comes back into play but for a brief moment you will have shown them what is possible, you will have enabled them to see how good they can feel.

'If you want to awaken all of humanity, then awaken all of yourself. If you want to eliminate all of the suffering in the world, then eliminate all that is dark and negative in yourself. Truly, the greatest gift you have to give is that of your own transformation'.

-Lao Tzu
Ancient Chinese philosopher and poet

—

Chapter 6

'Our thoughts can make us sick'
-Joe Dispenza
Neuroscientist, Lecturer and Author

Conclusion

So practicing the visualisation will enable you to become more aware of the way you think and feel, as well as teaching you what it feels like to be in the higher vibrations.

This in turn provides a positive anchor point that you can train yourself to quickly return to when negativity rears its ugly head.

And the added bonus is that following this practice of detaching from your negative emotions when they flare up, is that this will also release some of those emotions therefore enabling you to naturally start drifting upwards in vibration.

This is how you 'change yourself' or to put it another way 'love yourself' and loving yourself is how you start the process of creating the life you always wanted.

You see loving yourself is about getting rid of all the negativity inside of you that keeps you held down in vibration away from love.

As Rumi says you remove all the barriers you have built against love.

It's not about trying to like or appreciate yourself more while you are still carrying lot's of inner negativity because it will always infect and drown out your efforts, it's about removing the negativity then you will drift up in vibration to a place where you are naturally happier and more appreciative of yourself and your life.

Detachment from gremlin influenced negative surges is the key to a higher vibrational existence, an existence naturally filled with more self-love and appreciation in every sense of the word.

The current way that you are managing negativity by essentially giving it free reign in your life and fully engaging it every time it flares up is simply adding to its power and keeping you trapped in the lower vibrations where you will have much more of it to contend with. You are unknowingly through your programmed instinctive reactions keeping yourself stuck in the quagmire of negativity, which compounds any difficulties or challenges you may have to face.

And I believe this is the main factor behind the 'mental health crisis' that we are seeing sweeping across the world today.

Our gremlins have us trapped and we spend most of our time on the perpetual hamster wheel feeding them with our negative emotions, to all intents and purposes we have become a slave to the gremlin within. To move away from the majority of mental health problems we just have to work on releasing our trapped negative emotions and raise our vibration. In other words shrinking the gremlin is the way to salvation.

Surely this should be taught to our children (and everybody else) from an early age to empower them and give them the best possible chance in life? Please get behind this drive for humanity and if you can help in anyway to push this forward I can be contacted at **stevewharton23@aol.co.uk**

Also if you would be so kind as to leave a review for this book on Amazon I would be very grateful.

https://www.amazon.co.uk/This-Book-WILL-Change-Your/dp/B0B4DX6Q3L

Thank you
Steve Wharton

Chapter 7

'It is important to remember that you are vibrating a frequency every second. To change the outside circumstances and shift your life to a higher level, you must change the frequency on the inside of you.

Thoughts of goodness, words of goodness, and deeds of goodness lift your frequency higher.

The higher your frequency, the more good you bring to you'.

The Secret
-Rhonda Byrne

Rhonda Byrne is an Australian television writer and producer and the author of the best selling book 'The Secret'.

Manifesting

Your thoughts, feelings and emotions form your beliefs and what you believe is the driving force that manifests your life. You are essentially living in a belief driven universe.

So if you want something different change what you believe.

—
40

Sounds easy enough but the monkey wrench in the works is your inner negativity (your gremlin) which is having a massive negative influence independent of you. You have this alien force messing with your thoughts, feelings, emotions and ultimately beliefs.

It is possible if you can attain a feeling of peace and serenity to move up in vibration out of reach of the gremlin and for a while as long as you can hold the serene feelings manifest from there. And this is when you can really have some control over what you are manifesting (you are in the zone) but the gremlin will eventually come back into play and infect your results.

This is why it is so difficult to control what you want to manifest and as long as you carry this source of negativity you will always have mixed results. The answer is work on getting rid of the gremlin and as it shrinks your ability to manifest deliberately will improve accordingly. Following the inner lake practice and other methods to release your inner negativity will pay huge dividends in respect of empowering you with more control over what you want to manifest. The bottom line is you can actually manifest anything you want but until you get rid of the gremlin and get your vibration up you will struggle to find any consistency and have unreliable results.

—

To consistently see good results you have to force yourself up the vibrations and hold yourself there, which is very difficult to do for long when you are still carrying heavy slow vibrating energy within.

The answer is off load the negative energy then you will naturally rise up and stay there, then you will be able to exert much more control over what you are trying to manifest.

This is why books that promise to change your life without addressing the factor of your inner negativity often don't deliver.

You may even have some short term success but eventually it will be spoilt when your inner negativity comes back into play.

This is because your initial excitement, joy and eagerness at potentially finding the answer temporarily propels you up in vibration so you are manifesting from there but it won't be long before the pull from your inner gremlin drags you back down to your 'normal' vibrational level then its back to your usual less consistent results.

I expect many people have experienced this and can identify with a flurry of early success then inexplicably it fades away.

Now you know why.

Other recommended books and videos:

Feeding your demons, Author Tsultrim Allione, Hay House Publishing

The Power of Now, Author Eckhart Tolle, Namaste Publishing

The Emotion Code, Author Bradley Nelson, Penguin Publishing

Oneness, Author Rasha, Earthstar Press

The Secret, Author Rhonda Byrne, Thorsons/Simon & Schuster UK

High Vibrational Thinking, the power to change your life, Author Steve Wharton, Amazon Kindle

The most important years of a child's life, Author Steve Wharton, Amazon Kindle

Bullying Stops Here, Author Steve Wharton, Amazon Kindle

The Power of Non-resistance, Author Steve Wharton, Amazon Kindle

Videos:
E-motion the movie
www.e-motionthemovie.com

Facebook Community Page

Name: This Book WILL Change Your Life

Join our facebook community (group) and we will keep you updated with all the news and latest ideas. See how others are getting on and pick up tips on how to raise your vibration, what's working and what isn't.

The more people we can gather together the better and we will be giving away other books etc as we go along.

Let's raise the vibration together because the more people that join the more we can really have an impact.

Raising the vibration is often referred to as ascending and this is the goal, ascending into the higher vibrations, or rising up into love (the highest vibrating energy), which many ancient teachings refer to as rising up and coming into harmony with the energy of Christ Consciousness.

This is how we can play our part in changing the world into a better more loving and beautiful place.

https://www.facebook.com/groups/5662588 94992592

Printed in Great Britain
by Amazon

24253139R00026